The Duty of Scholars in the Absence of the Imām عَجَّلَ اللهُ تَعَالَى فَرَجَهُ الشَّرِيف

Āyatullāh Sayyid
Hādī Mudarrisī

AL-BURĀQ

Copyright

ISBN: 978-1-956276-22-0
Printed and published by al-Burāq Publications.
Translated and annotated by al-Burāq Publications. Where needed, context and transliterations were added. Some minor edits were made to the translated Arabic text.

Ordering Information
We offer discounts and promotions for wholesale purchases, non-profit organizations, and other educational institutions. Contact us at the email below for further information.

www.al-Buraq.org
publications@al-Buraq.org

First Edition | July 2022

Dedication

The publication of this book was made possible through the generous support of our donors.

Please recite *Sūrat al-Fātiha* and ask God for the Divine reward (*thawāb*) to be conferred upon the donors and also the souls of all the deceased in whose memory their loved ones have contributed graciously towards the publication of *The Duty of Scholars in the Absence of the Imām* عجل الله تعالى فرجه الشريف.

We begin by giving all praise and thanks to God ﷻ for giving us the tawfiq to translate this book. He has guided us and without Him, we would not have been guided to the straight path embodied by the Prophet Muḥammad ﷺ and the Ahl al-Bayt عليهم السلام.

This book is dedicated firstly to Āyatullāh Sayyid Hādī Mudarrisī, who made tremendous strides in advancing the cause of Islam. It is also dedicated to all the scholars, martyrs, and believers who worked tirelessly to promote the pure Muḥammadan path.

We want to also give our thanks and appreciation to all believers from around the world and acknowledge the team which helped al-Burāq Publications complete this work, spending countless hours to make its publication possible. Please recite Sūrat al-Fātiḥah on behalf of them, their families, and their marḥūmīn.

This book is dedicated in honor of the following individuals. Please remember them in your prayers and may God ﷻ have mercy on them and their loved ones.

Abrahim Ajami

Ali A. Ftouni

Ali Aoun

Alya Agemy

Aya Flayyih

Banday Khuda

Bano Rashida

Dalal Haoui

Hajj Ahmad Chit

Hajj Ali Hammoud

Hajj Amin Bakri

Hajj Haidar Alaouie

Hajj Hassan Sobh

Hajj Moslem Srour

Hajj Sami Ftouni

Hajji Amneh Sobh-Ftouni

Hajji Hiam Hojeije

Hajji Iman Elsaghir

Hajji Imane Srour

Hajji Miri Srour

Hajji Mounira Awad

Hajji Raidi Bazzi

Hajji Sobhia D. Aoun

Hassan Baker

Ibrahim Yazback

Izzat Aoun

Janna Berry

Kaniz Kubra

Khadije Aoun

Majeda Nasserdine

Meerna A. Aoun

Munawwar Jehan

Nawaz Rustami

Rochelle Johnson

Sayyid Sobh H. Sobh

Shafa Sayeed-Hussain

Shandar Fatima

Syed Mehdi Rizvi

Syed Nawaab Kazmi

Turfah Sobh

Victoria Yazback

Duʿāʾ al-Ḥujjah

اللهم كن لوليك الحجة بن الحسن صلواتك
عليه وعلى آبائه في هذه الساعة وفي كل
ساعة وليا وحافظا وقائدا وناصرا ودليلا
وعينا حتى تسكنه أرضك طوعا وتمتعه فيها طويلا

O God, be, for Your representative, the Ḥujjat (proof), son of al-Ḥasan, Your blessings be upon him and his forefathers, in this hour and in every hour: a guardian, a protector, a leader, a helper, a proof, and an eye - until You make him live on the Earth, in obedience (to You), and cause him to live in it for a long time.

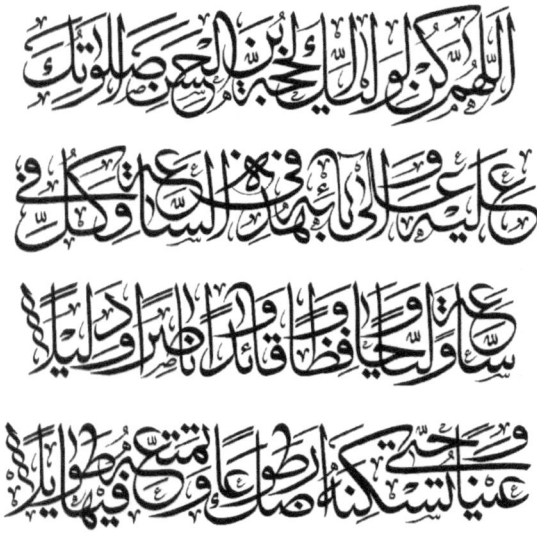

Terms of Respect

The following Arabic phrases have been used throughout this book in their respective places to show the reverence which the noble personalities deserve.

سبحانه وتعالى

Used for God, meaning:
Exalted and Sublime (Perfect) is He

ﷺ

Used for Prophet Muḥammad, meaning:
Blessings from God be upon him and his family

عليه السلام

Used for a man (singular) of a high status, meaning:
Peace be upon him

عليها السلام

Used for a woman (singular) of a high status, meaning:
Peace be upon her

عليهما السلام

Used for men/women (dual) of a high status, meaning:
Peace be upon them both

عليهم السلام

Used for men and/or women (plural) of a high status, meaning:
Peace be upon them all

عجل الله تعالى فرجه الشريف

Used for Imām Muḥammad al-Mahdī, meaning:
May God hasten his return

طاب ثراه

Used for a deceased scholar, meaning:
May his resting [burial] place remain pure

Transliteration Table

The method of transliteration of Islamic terminology from the Arabic language has been carried out according to the standard transliteration table below.

ء	ʾ	ر	r	ف	f
ا	a	ز	z	ق	q
ب	b	س	s	ك	k
ت	t	ش	sh	ل	l
ث	th	ص	ṣ	م	m
ج	j	ض	ḍ	ن	n
ح	ḥ	ط	ṭ	و	w
خ	kh	ظ	ẓ	ه	h
د	d	ع	ʿ	ي	y
ذ	dh	غ	gh		
Long Vowels					
ا	ā	و	ū	ي	ī
Short Vowels					
ـَ	a	ـُ	u	ـِ	i

Table of Contents

About the Author

Āyatullāh Sayyid Hādī Mudarrisī

Over the course of two generations and five decades, the Islamic world has known the personality of Āyatullāh Sayyid Hādī Mudarrisī – not through his writings, which exceed two hundred books, nor through his lectures, which exceeded eight thousand lectures alone, nor through his articles and words – instead, the Islamic world knows him for all of these matters and in addition to that, they know him for his social and political activities; up until his name become familiar. A name which brings comfort and tranquility to the heart, and enlightens the mind with awareness and insight.

Sayyid Hādī Mudarrisī exemplifies a religious scholar who combines knowledge, work, religion, the Message, thought and movement. The Islamic arena witnessed him – with his tireless *jihādī* activities in support of the oppressed and the underprivileged – resist tyrants and challenge their authority. Therefore, his generosity was not limited to one aspect over the other. On the contrary, for him, there was no door of knowledge that remained closed. This is what enabled him to present a rich culture in various religious, social, scientific, moral and civil affairs and issues.

With the help of God ﷻ, his eminence's literary ingenuity, his innovative and original outlook and his precision in expressing the core of Islamic thought, as well as his scientifically interesting style, allowed him to win the hearts of millions who read his work, listened to him, or attended his lectures and were drawn to his appealing behavior and virtuous manners. This was achieved through combining religious authenticity, scientific modernity and the rest of the necessities of the era; as his interesting and breathtaking style and modesty in all cases are among the features for which he was famous and what caused the hearts of the people to be drawn to him.

Intellectual and Scientific Contributions

Sayyid Hādī Mudarrisī is considered one of the prominent figures in the Islamic arena. He is also one of the leading scholars who carried the esteemed message of the Holy Prophet ﷺ. He is a thinker, orator, speaker, author and scholar of the contemporary Islamic Awakening flags. He began writing at a young age, and during the years of his life, he offered authentic Islamic thought that was suitable for the era the people were living in.

While atheism was plotting to hijack the sons of the Islamic nation, Sayyid Hādī Mudarrisī contradicted the ideas of atheists with his writings, and revealed Islam's power and ability to solve the problems of the world. When the issues increased, he focused on giving the people hope for the victory of Islam, since it is the best alternative mankind. When the conviction of the people solidified, he began to put forward detailed visions of Islam on various issues, where his writings amounted to almost two hundred books, studies and pamphlets. During this time, he made every effort to reform the Islamic Society and liberate them from the shackles of injustice and oppression that were and still are tightened around the neck of the ummah.

His Upbringing

Sayyid Hādī Mudarrisī was born in the year 1366 Hijri (1947 AD). He grew up in the city of Karbalā', 'Irāq, which holds the shrine of the prophet's grandson and his fragrance, Imām al-Ḥusayn عليه السلام. Sayyid Mudarrisī smelled the soil of Karbalā', drank from the Euphrates, and grew up in its embrace.

His Eminence comes from two families famous for science and virtue. On the paternal side, his late father, his Eminence Āyatullāh Sayyid Muḥammad Kāẓim Mudarrisī قدس سره, who was one of the leading scholars in the Islamic Seminary in the holy city of Mashhad and the city of Karbalā', and was one of the most prominent students of Āyatullāh Mīrzā Mahdī Gharawī Iṣfahānī قدس سره. He was also a competent teacher in the knowledge of the divine truth derived from the Noble Qur'ān and the *aḥadīth* of the Ahl al-Bayt عليهم السلام. He took his inspiration from Imām al-Mahdī عجل الله تعالى فرجه الشريف. His great-grandfather, His Eminence Āyatullāh Sayyid Muḥammad Bāqir Mudarrisī قدس سره, was one of the *marāji'* of Islam, and his older brother, His Eminence Āyatullāh Sayyid Muḥammad Taqī Mudarrisī, is also one of the current *marāji'*. He also has six other brothers, amongst them are jurists, competent teachers and verbal orators.

On the maternal side, he belongs to the family of Sayyid Shīrāzī, a family known as the religious authority in the Islamic world. His grandfather, His Eminence Āyatullāh Sayyid Mahdī Shīrāzī قدس سره, and his uncle, the late Āyatullāh Sayyid Muḥammad Shīrāzī قدس سره, as well as Āyatullāh Sayyid Ṣādiq Shīrāzī.

His other maternal uncle, His Eminence Āyatullāh Sayyid Ḥasan Shīrāzī قدس سره, was a scientist, A mujāhid, a brilliant writer, and a martyr who stood up to the tyrannical regime in ʿIrāq, until he was arrested, tortured, harmed, and finally assassinated in Beirut by the criminal Saddam, the tyrant of ʿIrāq. His Eminence Sayyid Ḥasan Shīrāzī قدس سره had a great impact on the personality of Sayyid Hādī Mudarrisī due to their closeness in terms of relationship, work and objectives.

Since his childhood, he grew up in the atmosphere of the Islamic Seminary in the holy city of Karbalāʾ, where he began his scientific studies at the age of thirteen, and completed the lessons of the advanced stages in the seminary, which is known as the highest stage of study in Islamic seminaries. Under the age of twenty-five, he was among the leading scholars of the city of Karbalā'.

It is noteworthy to mention that he passed his academic stages with great success and remarkable excellence, which caught the attention of his professors, since his Eminence was superior in his scientific position, and distinguished in his religious, cultural and social activities. Accordingly, he received the support of the leading religious authorities, and they granted him agency (*ijāzah*) regarding the authorization of accounts and distribution of the religious dues. Among these scholars are Āyatullāh Sayyid Muḥammad Shīrāzī ﷺ, Āyatullāh Sayyid Khumaynī ﷺ, Āyatullāh Sayyid Marʿashī Najafī ﷺ, and Āyatullāh Sayyid ʿAbd al-Aʿla Mūsawī Sabziwārī ﷺ. Due to his intense activity and the confidence of the scholars in him, and the desire to be a representative of them, they took the initiative to send their agencies to him without his permission; such as Sayyid Khumaynī ﷺ.

In his early twenties, he completed teaching introductory, intermediate, and advanced sciences, such as from the books *al-Kifāya* and *al-Rasā'il*. Prominent scientists, orators, authors and poets have graduated under his guidance.

While he was busy studying, he took part in cultural, political and social activities. He wrote in the local newspaper of the city of Karbalā', and also participated in its religious mass celebrations.

When the Communist wave spread in 'Irāq, His Eminence emerged to face this danger, and then he struggled since the Baathist rule in 'Irāq, especially after the ruling authority arrested a number of senior religious scholars such as Shahīd Sayyid Mahdī Ḥakīm ﵀ and Shahīd Sayyid Ḥasan Shīrāzī ﵀.

When he became endangered, he emigrated to Lebanon, and then to Kuwait. After that, he emigrated to Bahrain to exercise his responsibilities in managing the religious and cultural affairs of the people. He remained there until he became one of its flag bearers, and a leader with a mission. Hundreds of believers gathered around him for hist knowledge and work ethic, and the his civilized vision emanating from the spirit of the True Islam.

As a result of his active activities in Bahrain, he was deported to Iran after the Islamic Revolution. Thus he began a new start, filled with activity and efficiency.

Exile in Iran

Whilst in Iran, Sayyid Mudarrisī continued his activism and kept supporting the Bahraini population against the Āl Khalīfah regime. The IFLB came to prominence as the front organization for the 1981 coup, which attempted to install Sayyid Mudarrisī as the spiritual leader of a newly established theocratic Shīʿa state. However the coup failed, and so Sayyid Mudarrisī reorganized the structure of the Front, focusing on its information efforts in Europe.

Sayyid Mudarrisī became a founding member of the Supreme Council for the Islamic Revolution in ʿIrāq (SCIRI), and was among the active figures of the ʿIrāqi opposition in exile. He was closely involved in efforts to expose and bring down the regime in Baghdad. He managed to escape a number of assassination attempts abroad, including one in Brazil in 1991 as well as two more attempts in Syria, by the Bathist intelligence operatives, in 2001.

Return to 'Irāq

Upon returning to 'Irāq after the fall of Saddam's regime, he was greeted by over thirty thousand people in Baghdad, fifty thousand in Sadr City and a similar crowd in his hometown, Karbalā'.

Sayyid Mudarrisī established a television station upon his return to his hometown. He is also involved in several large-scale humanitarian projects in 'Irāq and has been involved in the building of mosques, schools, medical clinics, orphanages, and has been a staunch advocate of women's rights and consistently speaks out against the oppression of women in his lectures and books. He also facilitates marriage by providing financial help to people who wish to get married and has organized several large mass marriage ceremonies. Sayyid Mudarrisī also founded and currently heads the League of Religious Scholars which brings together many high ranking Shi'ite scholars or their representatives in 'Irāq.

Preface

بسم الله الرحمن الرحيم

In the Name of God, the Beneficent,
the Merciful

All praise belongs to God, Lord of all the worlds,

the Beneficent, the Merciful,

Master of the Day of Retribution.

You [alone] do we worship, and to You [alone] do we turn for help.

Guide us on the straight path, the path of those whom You have blessed

—such as have not incurred Your wrath, nor are astray.

What is the responsibility of scholars?

What are their rights?

Who are the scholars that must be followed?

Who are the scholars we must avoid?

What is the role that must be played by scholars in this age?

These questions, amongst others, are raised today, waiting to be answered. This book is an attempt to answer these questions by referring to the Holy Book of God and the Sunnah of his Noble Messenger ﷺ and immaculate Imāms عليهم السلام.

All success comes from God ﷻ and reliance is laid upon Him.

Āyatullāh Sayyid Hādī Mudarrisī

20 – Shawwal – 1400 AH

God ﷻ said in His Noble Book:

﴾*Certainly We sent Moses with Our signs: 'Bring your people out from darkness into light...*﴿[1]

God Almighty has spoken the truth.

---

[1] Sūrat Ibrāhīm, Verse 5.

Knowledge has a Message

The message of knowledge is to raise awareness and confer responsibility upon man.

Therefore, knowledge is a preamble rather than a conclusion. It is more of a cause than a goal.

Accordingly, Islam which considers knowledge a duty upon every Muslim, demands one to seek it even if it were in China. It also believes scholars to be better than the prophets of the sons of Israel, and describes the scholar who doesn't act upon his knowledge and forsakes it as a dog; for, it says:

﴾Relate *to them an account of him to whom We gave Our signs, but he cast them off*﴿[2]

And:

﴾*...So his parable is that of a dog: if you make for it, it lolls out its tongue, and if you let it alone, it lolls out its tongue...*﴿[3]

This is because knowledge is like a light which is used as a means of sight. Yet, what value does a

---

[2] Sūrat al-A'rāf, Verse 175.

[3] Sūrat al-A'rāf, Verse 176.

candle have if you do not use it to illuminate your path?

What value does a tree possess when it does not give you any fruit? And what is the value of the eye through which you do not see life?

ʿĪsā ibn Mariam ﷺ says:

"In truth I say to you: the worst of people is a knowledgeable man who preferred his worldly life over his knowledge, such that he loved it, demanded it and strived for it; and if he had to set people to confusion he would have. Yet, how does the amplitude of sunlight benefit a blind man who cannot see it? Likewise, a knowledgeable man does not benefit from the riches of his knowledge if he doesn't act upon it. Therefore, beware of hypocritical scholars whose words do not match their actions."[4]

---

[4] al-Ḥarrānī, Ibn Shuʿba, *Tuḥaf al-ʿUqūl*, p. 375.

The Responsibility of Scholars

The question raised here is: What is the responsibility of scholars?

The answer is: Scholars carry two main responsibilities:

First: Their responsibility towards the people.

Second: Their responsibility towards the rulers.

Regarding their responsibility towards the people, it is summed up as follows:

1. Reminding People of their Obligations and Responsibilities.

﴾*So* admonish—*for* you *are only an admonisher*﴿[5]

Imām Jaʿfar al-Ṣādiq ﷺ says: "If you are informed of a man of despicable misconduct, what prevents you from approaching him, scolding and advising him, and addressing him with eloquent speech."[6]

---

[5] Sūrat al-Ghāshiyah, Verse 21.

[6] Majlisī, ʿAllāma Muḥammad Bāqir, *Biḥār al-Anwār*, Vol. 10, p. 86.

2. Raising Public Awareness, Disclosing Truths and Clarifying the Permissible (Halāl) and Impermissible (Harām) Acts.

Imām ʿAlī عليه السلام says: "God did not establish a covenant with ignorant people which mandates that they pursue the quest of knowledge, until he established a covenant with the people of knowledge which mandates that they clarify knowledge to the ignorant; for, knowledge precedes ignorance."[7]

Imām Jaʿfar al-Ṣādiq عليه السلام says: "In every century, this religion carries just individuals who refute the (false) interpretations of the nullifiers thereof, the distortions of the exaggerators, and the hypocrisy of the ignorant, just as the bellows remove impurities from iron."[8]

3. Instilling Hope in the Hearts of People.

Imām ʿAlī عليه السلام says: "Shall I tell you of a true jurist? It is the person who does not make

---

[7] Majlisī, ʿAllāma Muḥammad Bāqir, *Biḥār al-Anwār*, Vol. 2, p. 23.

[8] *Rijāl al-Kāshi*, p. 4.

people hopeless of God's mercy, nor makes them feel safe from His torment, nor makes them despaired of His clemency, nor permits or tolerates acts that disobey Him."[9]

4. Working for the Sake of the Poor and Deprived, and Eliminating the Oppression that Befalls Them.

Imām 'Alī ﷺ says: "God took upon scholars to refrain from being silent about the fullness (extravagance) of an oppressor and the hunger of the oppressed."[10]

Imām Ja'far al-Ṣādiq ﷺ also says: "Some scholars see it fit to place knowledge at the disposal of the wealthy and noble; whereas they do not find a place for it at the table of the poor. These (scholars) will be placed in the third depths of the Hellfire."[11]

---

[9] Ḥurr al-'Āmilī, Shaykh Muḥammad ibn al-Ḥasan, *al-Wasā'il*, Vol. 4, p. 830.

[10] Sharīf Raḍī, Muḥammad ibn al-Ḥusayn, *Nahj al-Balāgha*, Sermon/Letter/Saying 52.

[11] Majlisī, 'Allāma Muḥammad Bāqir, *Biḥār al-Anwār*, Vol. 2, p. 108.

5. Enjoining Goodness and Forbidding Evil.

Imām Muḥammad al-Jawād ﷺ says: "Scholars are – themselves – traitors if they withhold advice, see a lost and misguided person yet refrain from guiding him, or see a dead person and refrain from covering him up. Woe to their misconduct; for, God took a pledge from them in the Noble Qur'ān to enjoin goodness and that which they were ordered ..., to forbid that which they were forbidden from, to cooperate in piety and God-wariness, and to refrain from cooperation in sin and aggression."[12]

---

[12] Kulaynī, Shaykh Muḥammad ibn Ya'qūb, *al-Kāfī*, Vol. 8, p. 54.

As for the scholars' responsibility towards the oppressive rulers, it lies in confrontation, resistance and battle.

God ﷻ says to His Prophet Mūsā عليه السلام

﴿*Go ahead, you and your brother, with My signs and do not flag in My remembrance. Let the two of you go to Pharaoh. Indeed he has rebelled*﴾[13]

And He ﷻ says:

﴿*...Then fight the leaders of unfaith —indeed they have no [commitment to] pledges...*﴾[14]

---

[13] Sūrat Ṭā Ḥā, Verses 42-43.

[14] Sūrat al-Tawbah, Verse 12.

The Qualities of Revolutionary Scholars

Scholars are of three types:

First: Revolutionary scholars

Second: Idle Scholars

Third: Dissolute Scholars

What are the qualities of the revolutionary scholars?

The answer is as follows:

1. Sacrifice for the Sake of God

For the resisting scholar neither fears death nor dreads to be killed.

Imām al-Ḥusayn ﷺ says: "If you were patient with the harm inflicted upon you and endured the burdensome expenses for the sake of God, then God's affairs would reach you, rise from you and return to you. However, if you allowed the oppressors to have power over you; and you placed God's affairs in their hands, whereby they committed suspicious acts and walked in the paths of lust, your fleeing from death gave them this power, in addition to your admiration for life which is leaving you."[15]

Imām Muḥammad al-Jawād ﷺ says: "God placed - within scholars - remains from all the prophets preceding them... so that they would guide those who go astray towards righteousness and summon (people) towards God. Thus, look towards them; for, they have a high position even if they were inflicted with low-grade circumstances in this world. Through the book of God, they bring the dead back to life. And through His light, they give the blind back their sight. How many of Satan's victims have they brought back to life? And how many lost and misguided souls have they guided? They sacrifice their own blood to save the people. And what great influence they have on the people."[16]

---

[15] al-Ḥarrānī, Ibn Shuʿba, *Tuḥaf al-ʿUqūl*, p. 172.

[16] Kulaynī, Shaykh Muḥammad ibn Yaʿqūb, *al-Kāfī*, Vol. 2, p. 56.

2. Bravery

A revolutionary scholar is a brave man who fears none but God ﷻ.

God ﷻ says:

﴾Such as deliver the messages of God and fear Him, and fear no one except God, and God suffices as reckoner﴿[17]

And He says:

﴾Only those of God's servants having knowledge fear Him﴿[18]

It is clear that he who fears God ﷻ alone doesn't fear or dread anyone.

The sacred hadith says: "He who fears God, God makes everything fear him.. And he who doesn't fear God, God makes him afraid of everything." (The word of God)

---

[17] Sūrat al-Aḥzāb, Verse 39.

[18] Sūrat Fāṭir, Verse 28.

3. Humbleness towards People

A revolutionary scholar is like a full tree whose branches bow down as their fruits increase.

The Prophet ﷺ says: "He who pursues knowledge for the sake of God establishes more humility within himself and with people, more fear of God and more jurisprudence in religion with every chapter he covers. It is he who benefits from knowledge; therefore, let him learn it."[19]

The Prophet ʿĪsā ibn Mariam ﵇ said: "In truth I say to you: plants grow in the valley and do not grow on a mountaintop. Likewise, wisdom thrives in a humble heart and does not thrive in the heart of a harsh and arrogant person. Don't you know that he who raises his head up to the ceiling damages it, and he who lowers his head under it sits in its shade... Similarly, he who does not humble himself for God, God lowers his status. And he who humbles himself for God, God lifts him up."[20]

---

[19] *Rawdat al-Wāʾiẓin*, p. 11.

[20] al-Ḥarrānī, Ibn Shuʿba, *Tuḥaf al-ʿUqūl*, p. 375.

4. Asceticism

A revolutionary scholar is ascetic in the remains of this world.

The Prophet ﷺ says: "A man is not said to be a jurist unless he does not care which garment he wears... and with what he has satiated his hunger."[21]

5. Benefiting Others

A revolutionary scholar sees himself as the great Sayyid Khumaynī saw himself: a mere servant for the people.

Imām Muḥammad al-Bāqir says: "A scholar whose knowledge benefits people is better than seventy worshippers."[22]

---

[21] Majlisī, ʿAllāma Muḥammad Bāqir, *Biḥār al-Anwār*, Vol. 2, p. 49.

[22] Kulaynī, Shaykh Muḥammad ibn Yaʿqūb, *al-Kāfī*, Vol. 1, p. 33.

The Qualities of Dissolute Scholars

Knowledge is like a weapon which can be held by either a faithful believer or a dissolute hypocrite. The believer uses it in favor of righteousness; and the dissolute man uses it in support of falsehood.

What are the qualities of dissolute scholars?

The answer is:

1. Abandoning Awareness-Raising

A dissolute scholar neither spreads knowledge nor fulfills the obligation of raising awareness.

The Prophet ﷺ says: "He who conceals beneficial knowledge, God binds him on the day of Resurrection with chains of fire."[23]

Imām Ja'far al-Ṣādiq ﵇ says:

"Some of the scholars love to store their knowledge and prefer not to share it with

---

[23] Majlisī, 'Allāma Muḥammad Bāqir, *Biḥār al-Anwār*, Vol. 2, p. 78.

others. These scholars will be placed in the first depth of the Hellfire."[24]

2. Love of this World

The dissolute scholar loves the worldly life and seeks it.

God ﷻ says:

﴾*Relate to them an account of him to whom We gave Our signs, but he cast them off. Thereupon Satan pursued him, and he became one of the perverse. Had We wished, We would have surely raised him by their means, but he clung to the earth and followed his [base] desires*﴿[25]

God ﷻ says:

﴾*O you who have faith! Indeed many of the scribes and monks wrongfully eat up the people's wealth, and bar [them] from the way of God*﴿[26]

[24] Majlisī, 'Allāma Muḥammad Bāqir, *Biḥār al-Anwār*, Vol. 2, p. 108.

[25] Sūrat al-A'rāf, Verses 175-176.

[26] Sūrat al-Tawbah, Verse 34.

Imām Ja'far al-Ṣādiq ﷺ says: "If you see a scholar in love with this world, blame him in the name of religion; for, every lover surrounds his beloved."

Imām Mūsā al-Kāẓim ﷺ says: "God conveyed to Dawūd: 'Tell my servants not to have a scholar, who is charmed with this world, standing in between Me and them; whereby he hinders them from My remembrance and from the path of My love and supplication. Those are the road blockers that keep my servants away from Me."[27]

3. Hypocrisy

A hypocritical scholar speaks words that please people, yet acts according to his desire.

The Prophet ﷺ said: "Woe to those who pursue this worldly life by using religion. They put on the disguise of an innocent lamb from the softness of their tongues. Their words are

[27] al-Ḥarrānī, Ibn Shu'ba, *Tuḥaf al-'Uqūl*, p. 29.

sweeter than honey and their hearts resemble the heart of a wolf."[28]

4. The Pursuit of Leadership

A dissolute scholar loves leadership and boasting.

The Prophet ﷺ says: "He who pursues knowledge to attract people's attention towards him doesn't realize the fragrance of Heaven."[29]

---

[28] Majlisī, ʿAllāma Muḥammad Bāqir, *Biḥār al-Anwār*, Vol. 77, p. 173.

[29] Ṭabrisī, Shaykh al-Faḍl ibn Ḥasan, *Makārim al-Akhlāq*, p. 541.

5. Cozying Up to Princes and Sultans (Men of Power)

God ﷻ says:

﴾*Have you not regarded those who were given a share of the Book believing in idols and the Rebels and saying of the pagans: 'These are better guided on the way than the faithful'? They are the ones whom God has cursed, and whomever God curses, you will never find any helper for him.*﴿[30]

The Prophet ﷺ says: "Beware of (standing at) the doors of the sultans and their surroundings; for, the closest ones amongst you thereto are the furthest from God. And he who prefers the sultan to God, God eliminates his piety and renders him confused."[31]

Imām Ja'far al-Ṣādiq ؑ says: "The Messenger of God ﷺ said: Scholars are the trustees of messengers as long as they do not immerse themselves in the worldly life. He was asked: O' Messenger of God, what immerses them in the

---

[30] Sūrat al-Nisā', Verses 51-52.

[31] *Thawāb al-A'māl*, p. 310.

worldly life? He ﷺ said: Following the sultan. If they do so, beware of them and be protective of your religion from them."[32]

6. Remaining Silent about Righteousness

A dissolute scholar is indifferent towards the happenings around him.

Imām al-Ḥusayn ﷣ says: "O' people, learn from God's advice to his followers and from his criticism of the priests when He said:

﴾*Why do not the rabbis and the scribes forbid them from sinful speech...*﴿[33]

And He ﷻ said:

﴾*The faithless among the Children of Israel were cursed...*﴿[34],

---

[32] Kulaynī, Shaykh Muḥammad ibn Ya'qūb, *al-Kāfī*, Vol. 2, p. 42.

[33] Sūrat al-Mā'idah, Verse 63.

[34] Sūrat al-Mā'idah, Verse 78.

And He ﷻ said:

﴾...*Evil is what they had been doing.*﴿[35]

Indeed, God considered this as a disgrace. For, they have witnessed vice and corruption from the people who lived amongst them and yet they haven't forbidden them from acting in this way, out of desire for that which they have been gaining from them and fear of what they dread might happen.

God ﷻ says:

﴾*So do not fear the people, but fear Me*﴿[36]

7. Promoting Division

A dissolute scholar loves division and instigates conflicts.

---

[35] Sūrat al-Mā'idah, Verse 79.

[36] al-Ḥarrānī, Ibn Shuʿba, *Tuḥaf al-ʿUqūl*, p. 171.

God ﷻ says:

❨*They did not divide [into sects] except after the knowledge had come to them, out of envy among themselves*❩[37]

Imām 'Alī ؑ describes evil scholars by saying: "One of them comes across a case which seeks his ruling and he rules according to his opinion. Then, the same case is presented to another person who provides a different ruling. Thus, the judges gather for a meeting with the Imām who appointed them as judges; and he aligns all their opinions. And they all have the same one God, one prophet and one book."

"Did God ﷻ order them to have conflicting opinions whereby they have obeyed Him? Or did He forbid them from that whereby they disobeyed Him?"[38]

---

[37] Sūrat al-Shūrā, Verse 14.

[38] Sharīf Raḍī, Muḥammad ibn al-Ḥusayn, *Nahj al-Balāgha*, Sermon/Letter/Saying 74.

8. Practicing Debauchery

A dissolute scholar has no piety.

Imām ʿAlī ﷺ says: "Beware of the ignorant worshippers and the dissolute scholars... For, they are the source of disturbance for every troubled person."[39]

And he ﷺ says: "I lost my backbone to two men in this world: a dissolute man who has a knowledgeable tongue and a worshiper who has an ignorant heart. Beware of the dissolute man from amongst the scholars; for, I heard the Messenger of God ﷺ say: The destruction of my nation will be at the hands of every dissolute man who has a knowledgeable tongue."[40]

Imām Jaʿfar al-Ṣādiq ﷺ says: "In the Hellfire, there exists a mill which grinds five types of people, won't you ask me what it grinds? ... He was asked, "And what does it grind?" He said,

---

[39] Majlisī, ʿAllāma Muḥammad Bāqir, *Biḥār al-Anwār*, Vol. 2, p. 106.

[40] *Rawḍat al-Wāʿiẓin*, p. 6.

"dissolute scholars, dissolute readers, oppressive tyrants, disloyal ministers and lying mystics."[41]

The Prophet ﷺ was asked: "Who are the worst of people? He said: scholars, if they become corrupt."[42]

Those were the qualities of the scholars, the revolutionary and the dissolute. What, then, is the required stance towards each of them?

The answer is as follows.

The Messenger of God ﷺ provided a brief summary of this stance by saying: "Do not sit at the table of every pretentious caller (towards Islam) who invites you away from certainty towards doubt, from humbleness towards arrogance, from advice towards enmity, and from asceticism towards desire.

And establish proximity towards a scholar who invites you away from arrogance towards

---

[41] Ṣadūq, Shaykh Muḥammad ibn 'Alī, *al-Khiṣāl*, Vol. 2, p. 142.

[42] al-Ḥarrānī, Ibn Shu'ba, *Tuḥaf al-'Uqūl*, p. 31.

humbleness, from insincerity towards sincerity, from doubt towards certainty, from desire towards asceticism, and from enmity towards advice."[43]

In a nutshell:

The required stance towards the revolutionary scholars is obeying them and following their footsteps. Whereas the stance towards the idle scholars is leaving them and keeping distance from them.

As for the stance towards the dissolute scholars, it would be in exposing them and confronting them so that they do not misguide the servants of God ﷻ.

[43] Majlisī, ʿAllāma Muḥammad Bāqir, *Biḥār al-Anwār*, Vol. 2, p. 52.

www.ingramcontent.com/pod-product-compliance
Lightning Source LLC
Chambersburg PA
CBHW031258120626
46545CB00007B/2872
9781956276220